Dandelions That have Held your Breath.

poems and selected writing by

mikl paul.

Dedicated to all my friends and family

who have put up with years of these little dreams.

And foremost; To BreEle, my Queen, for teaching me

what all of this is for.

~

"Just once I wanted a task that required all the joy I had."

-Annie Dillard

I drink things like water
   and wonder at what airs
   you divide with how
you laugh.   loving, that
   you have become
a country and that I
   have become
      an accent.
when I ask your name
      to mountains,
   when it opens my heart
 and allows all to express;
the ocean answers for the
   silent heights; the
depths are grateful for
   the description of
clouds you write across
   your back before you
   swim.

there this the plain faced, this thisness

   of the small of my voice, the matches

won't strike and the light held against me.

   where one places the worth of it,

bottles every lasting drop,   what we are

   ready to finally know.   for the all

is well   our all is our.   and the wind

   of chorus bends our backs.

when the tower stayed the same,

     the city removing, the parking lot

   just beginning to empty.   the all that

paced beyond our sight, where

   your touch is just this, this

beyond our sight.

    and can you read this

   have you prayed have you wished

     does this want sing itself

to sleep

             or awake.

and these shells,   you see

   my hand here,   these *broken pieces*,

can you.   I mean.   can we?

in my fathers home we have these many rooms,

   but how close do you want to stand?

  hand poised, hope poised, mid-belief down to

a white knuckle faith and you know, (as close as

     we can) the heart has never been a retreat,

for

the first time, all of these strangers and pilgrims,

            and *your still small*

voice   and

     is any of this bearable?

there, still there is this unending that draws

us

toward our pale contours of becoming;

       the two of us, with one

    missing, just the two, but barely,

    but one is still missing, and the looking

  and the fine whisper of our vision easing

every answer.

coaxing, breakingly kind, hold the candle

until

  it is lit.   and with silhouette

revealing how all

   once was a once, and heartbreak and is any

  of this still bearable?   testing the waters

gently

   are you watching. turning anothers

directions

    are you watching?   there must be a witness to

the exhaust,   while she is staring

        while he has uncovered his shadow

against

        the cement sky,

           and it must be cold,   she is,

crying,

           and was this still my story?

   in this morning, in this season, where

should

    I return these things of elseone, where

would

    I even begin to kneel, to slide my legs, inch at

a static inch,

    just to see if oh god merely a story,

        barely, what must empty for

what to fill,   what you have displaced;

dreaming

   of this hallway,   and the warmth,

threatened

   by every open door.

There was once a boy, a very strange enchanted boy and we all have so much to learn from love if we are going to survive these days, or deserve to. There is a gentle here that I would like to find, there are places so near for our cleansing to aftershine and if this is your face turning to my face let the heart tell you why, let me tell you why, and there are all these reasons.

They must have organized each end with a new beginning somewhere holy and sacred; beneath sheets, beneath him, beneath her, they must have chosen to swallow that silk story and announce the death so sudden. And she says, I didn't mean to break your heart and he knows, and of course he knows, but, standing there so stained, and he replies You didn't break my heart, you only broke my dream, and we have to listen to their silence now hidden behind these heaving destinies, and we have to hope that some still hand is holding all of these shatterings, so still. But children still, run with arms wide and life is so loud when it begins and here we are.

They had lived in Grass Valley for two years before he ever wrote on her. He was always inside her, in one form or another. And there is a beauty there. But they had lived in Grass Valley for two years and one night, her back to his chest, he began to write about being within her, while he was within her, upon her; across skin in small black letters he told the sonnet of and they know that some things never happen again, and there are goldens collapsing upon us constantly, wave after wave of *surprise me surprise me* and together their eyes go wide, at themselves, at the enormous bell of core striking core and life is for important things. They promise, and

Who would I tell if not for you? I've tracked your mirage across an America of mirages and remember the first night after it wasn't the right door, yet it was your door, and somehow I never found the other door, and your door was the right door, and hello my name is, and eyes dark like my eyes dark and hair dark like my hair dark and I have whiskey you have wine and our mouths were so thick tasting when all of this lightness began. Your neighbor listened to music even though he was deaf, and yes.

Later when the lists enveloped what we were attempting to keep so free, we saved things from drowning by teaching them to love these shadows and to sing the moonlight down to you with a soul that is bright and is vibrant and is a witness. Because life is for things to be important. And somehow in the wreckage of what was left behind we built this sanctuary, we found this pair of eyes that we could hold our honests in and there is nothing greater than a life that is kept secret by a life that is kept secret and to the song of these dear borders fading we spoke with new tongues, and memorized the long road home.

They spent a summer talking beneath the redwoods. There was a curiosity to the way they knew. She would take his hips in her hands and turn him to the left, so the sun would not be in his eyes. He would take her hips in his hands and turn her to the right, so the sun would not be in her eyes.. It is a dance. A very careful way they care.

Somewhere elsewhere I imagine the sound of two bare hands. There would be steeples and something to write with. I would ask questions. At the end of that story there would be something tearing down, across the face, brief, and hurried, and a tone would change... an accent would announce not today, but the yesterday still lodged in it's blood, but for the first time, it would be noticed.

The way that some splendids are so ghostlike in the way they weave through us. In the ever present hollow of these chests something glistens and coos. Have you kept your pockets clean asks the fading daylight sheathing above the insisting hills and we aren't sure sometimes.. we have tried of course but there are roadblocks here, occasionally one must tread through wild lands and wild hearts to find the way around, and things break there, in the valley of those nights, it's always been difficult to feel innocent when you know that at least once in your life you were guilty of shedding innocent love.

I remember when my father retired and how much peace he had when he realized what he had stored away would be enough.. And I wonder where they store all of this intent? There are peninsulas abound and this scream that is holy and is pure has wanderlust and the determination of an earth quake. There was that morning she turned her face to his face and they swore to never step away again, that every logical warning to restrain the outflow of love and wonder was a lie and a dangerous one. If something is going to shine, they held, let it shine now.

Yet all around them was a sea of pages torn too swiftly. They recognized that there are wounds, here, between and upon them. You should have seen the eden hands they brought to bear with the patience of caverns and mothers. Life glowed itself backward and forgave erosion and disasters, they had arrived here, together, they could not hate the path that led them to each other, for what truly is waiting, when it's what you have been waiting for?

She was a bartender a few nights a week. He worked with his hands, early and outside. When those hours came and they found themselves alone they would think of not being alone. But never with a longing. Almost as a visit, to an old companion who sang solo beside you and all the while knew it was merely the intro. He left her a note in her right slipper that said when I was alone yesterday I was happy, and I wanted you to know. Because look at how much you've done in me.

The way you can leave a gentleness in the paths of those we love. The anticipation, the joy. Of watching, and suddenly, as though by ambush, someone beams. They littered the house with kindness and surrounded one another, in the best of ways. They both knew, to truly both know. Years before, when it began, but only barely, he asked her if he could write her, that there was something new that needed to be told, and he asked if he could use her voice, her face, her courage, her shape, and self, to tell their story before it came to pass, or did not, and she said yes. What do you imagine belief looks like? Do you think you would notice it in an eye or a walk? I'd like to believe so.

Bodies bend with the courtship that the day ripens in context and sweat. There is a giving here, they are so generous with each other, an extravagant oh I insist. He would taste her every morning and try to guess her dreams. She would often dream of the mornings when he would taste her and try to guess her dreams. They welcomed themselves.

There was a funeral, their first together, and it wasn't someone overly close but goodbyes always make people overly close. The anecdotes were heartbreakingly dull and after so many sighs he tells her he will write an entire book about loving her. Dreamlike, smoke and water and perfect. After the funeral they went to the hospital to look at the newborns, then the train station, it only felt right.

There is a deep truth in being at home enough with someone to kiss them while your lips are dry. And happiness may not be the greatest of things to hear, but it should be. What love can build is sturdy and collect what you came here for, undone splinter of the better place. Watch the orbit they fashion through the myth and the come of being human and being grateful for these dusts of history and dusts of letting go. If you were in their place could you say you would do any different? If you were to tally the halves of moons and the betrayals of angels you would leap just as surely. They only had what they are holding in the other ones hands.

and I've waited,

   as though suddenly

and then   and

   yes,

patiently   sudden.

    as   though

the entire story,

as though

really   has

it   been

keeping?   yes.

   keeping   every

suddenly.

there   distant

   watch   and

it begins

suddenly   as

lightly   as

   kept.

I have waited to

   be kept,   and

     you.

and you may be a bird, or

   the elusive star of day, through

this half-life revealing, a whole becoming

   warming my skin,   but *not of*

our body you read, not of a

   gathered loss do we weigh

against the grand before:

    but wading into the newness of

   miracles and their sway of motion.

when the segments collide, we surpass

   the one of webbing of our, is,

swept away   and you taste

of the memory of god abandoned.

    but where does this poem want

to hold us now? where has a single   breath

   been left unadored?

they glisten at every opportunity to welcome themselves.

    tell us all, when you arrive,   what the salt

    took from your skin in the sea   or

    the sweat he took in seas   or

                           what the salt

had become when you wring your glossy dreams

   and when you arrive will you share. maybe

   the flute isn't for you,   and maybe your chest

     is against mine but maybe this isn't for us

but.   brace. arm extend, weight. lip

   bite, barely.   she bites her own lip,

       barely, eyes crashing   like

  matches extinguished in an open palm,

and   she can't let anyone know   and

  he knows   and   his   finding

    echoes along the line of jaws and

                       what the salt

preserved   while you believe in the sea

   and his clench now,   sheets creasing

like starfish playing sad   and the chandelier

  slicks with condensation offered upward

by his moan and deargod what may be watching

  from the oldest gardens within us, what may

stare outward and investigate these mornings

  spent building a means with come and with

trust. the ghosts read their future in the smudge

of her left hand   pressed   against the wall,

as she rose above him,   hand to mouth,

-every wind given peacefully- and began to map

with her thighs what will be found upon

the rainforests of her breasts.

He paced beside some half waking and her eyelids were all he remembers of the map yet he knows his north and his purpose. She has unkept the flare of her chrysalis and trace the steps, and bend down slowly to palm the crooked grass or misplaced stone; she has dreamt this way before. Maybe they will only find one another by being somewhere they have never been and maybe none of this has a thing to do with forgiveness but home doesn't always resemble the path. If you don't believe us, ask the stars, or the remnant of every sincere love that you feel gathering upon your pallet.

Did they take the time to understand what they were attempting to do with the other? The ballast of this romance rings it's drum through the afterlove, there is only one name his fossil is the echo of... but cross the sea, they found it, picture them, late into their elder years, bent with the worth of a life upon their shoulders, staring out that window while the ink begins to dry and what they discovered there may only be described from there and such are the bountiful reasons that line the edges of young lovers; they know that everything grows.

But we haven't reached these depths merely to describe the darkness of becoming enfolded. No one returns empty handed in the end, regret is always available and willing. But if he wrote the path to there while here and they chose the now of it to consecrate the then, as a tribute, or monument or song, than life has made it clear that there is so much more to us than we ever expected to be loved.

When he wanted to touch her there was a fruit that wanted to be truth and every arc of beneath his hand bracing with fragrance strength lingered on the tip of his fingers as he tongued them dry.

When his mouth finds what mouths are for finding she holds her breasts to save them for him. She collects colors behind her eyelids that form as swans or branches rising.

There is a constellation forming in the light of his tongue within her. The city they are building asks you to stay; remind yourself what is worth keeping, while the lighthouse of your moan warns the ship of your heart that he is a stone.

Her hair is dark and he is watching. The upper window is being filled and the earthquake of her throat striking so near the danger of this is my heart and you are making it come and vulnerability is a beauty and I give this broken air and clench and your swallow and the upper window is being filled by captured dreams of static that you surely came here for.

She looks to the left of the moments and the right and again she has dreamt this way before; the residue bleeds familiar and the things her hands have touched and the places she has left behind, after realizing that she knew what this was and loved what this was but was unable to remember what it was when she first arrived here and how long has it been since you knew you were known and to settle in that season and allow your heart to grow, and not always heal heal heal heal?

Some of these are for hearing. Some of them are for a word to be said and to be said true. Some of these braveries have been wasted. But the only true innocence of a story is at the beginning; at the end, one way or another, someone has always lost, and someone has always gained. But they never spoke that way. They spoke of meteors striking at the thought. They spoke of rainwater attempting to touch everything.

Later when they would mention, they would say, and everyone would know, but not nearly as well as they meant.

She had this window. He had these mouthfuls of curiosity. There was a brimming they adored and shaped from ideal and flesh, a forest of the heart swollen with the wildlife of their fear and sincerity.

I imagine her getting things ready, I see her setting things free.

And she talks to herself. Choosing to just love one person, she says, has an inherit honor within it, because you are saying no to the chance of every other love.

Not to the loves, themselves, she thinks, but to the chance. To the beginnings and much of this story has arced and mourned the loss of so many lovers. Life it seems is a parable of loves that failed until a love named pure arrives.

I remember the first hitchhiking trip and I was seventeen and so brave and we found the abandoned avocado ranch being squatted by a few dozen gutter punks and there were these walks we would take and guards we would set and the horse we fed back to life and the freedom of being free and the sturdy breaths as we built the compost heap. As we added to what we were changing into our own. While my heart was being romanced by the gem of this life, a heart so new and still so radiant, I remember realizing that everything can be your own. That this is what there was, there was this space and the faces that face each other and if you.are.going.to.do.one.damn.thing in your entire life let it be for love and I have been loved by people that were half dream and half sea, amazing incredible beams, and it honors me. Because when all things are your own for the shaping and one other character in this shabby house of a life decides they want to make this world with you, there should be an honor worthy of the poem that is the word creation.

And when she turns her face he basks and there is this wind they can't wait to love to. She looks upward and there is place on the brim of her neck that sings whisper. There are these myths they tongue in the afternight when along some quiet dreamcity wall, their shadows can be seen leaping down into the taller grass; he jumps first and catches her, everytime.

They know that life is for important things. They shove their hands down deep and with eyes wide, they stare, palm open and revealed and ask do you love what I have found, would you mind if we spent the remainder of these days learning how to stay gentle in the midst of so much new?

I remember reading about them;

how love is a massive thing. she would

emerge from the light into another light, and call

for him. he would surface from every dreamscape

and respond. –and all is tenderness.-

there was a kindness

in the way they drove one another, to one another.

I want to believe in the overflow you

    offer me. would you mind if this

          captured light was released

        gradually   because I

         celebrate you.

I want to gossip about forever

     against the part of your back that is

mine.

we could hear two voices and we could

    be them and the earth slants so

  yellow and she loves that he is a language

     and let the salt of it bristle;

     tongued. concave gentle and shedding

     skin and wishing and what

it is that we love that we are doing.

when the hum rises and remakes astrology

    I will sing between your singing and

    name this with me; I will pretend I am a

    hunter and you pretend to be

       the forest he knows.

when what we wanted was for

   us both to know.   and I both know.

and. warmth. beckon linger.

   you are your splendid;   just

let it –again but quiet- aghast, your

mouth is open,   wreck the hurried

   heartstop and to find it, here

after all this time,   there,   to

find it; what is waiting when it

   is what you have been waiting for?

so   warmth escapes the bright

   word of your words and I keep it.

I need you a symphony and you are restiform; the fable lowered from the highest window. I don't know if I have ever truly believed that everyone deserves love. But if I had to take it one moment further into those shadowed valleys of heartfull, I would admit that I do believe that love, deserves everyone. Now, watch him begin to climb.

Everytime he is inside her, there is a timelessness, a prophetic raising; he will always be inside her. And within that glimpse as who they are accomplishing what who they will be will continue to accomplish, there are reservoirs and storehouses they are able to access though they have yet to create. Would you like to gather me? I have these shines that live through my face and aren't we tired of pretending that when we make love it is with our bodies?

She has this bird cage beneath her ribs and his tongue can calm the static. There is a depiction above the height of an old bed frame in a home once theirs that confesses in broken brail the journey of these mines. If you stand across the room when the sun rose like it did those times and if you were as quiet as shadows mourning you may have heard the small beginning of something important. He was asleep and she hadn't been there long, in this place, but she lays there and watched him breath and she has these hurts from reckless hands and she knows the warnings of her mind and experience but yet he is new and he isn't what has been and in some center flare she chooses to never allow the time stolen to prevent her from giving again. She decides the heart is unable to be given in sections. He woke up not long after, and she said What would you like to do today and he says everything and while she watches him get dressed she wonders about things like sinking ships and compartments of air, and she smiles.

I would like to harness them for their own sake. If, imagine, them, standing, face to face, touching, and how the world must go through him to find her, and how the world must go through her to find him, and I would lay them down that way, to watch them strive upon the other so patiently, in no hurry, for they are already where they would like to be.

You are the raindance above me. Count the seasons with excitement, as though they may change. When the dusk is a child that interrupts out of wonder, when they came asking for you by name and you were ripe. I have swollen all of these rememberings and still nothing seems familiar.

He had written things. There were papers piled on the counter top and when she got home he was still on his way and she read what he wrote and never told him. When love wants to live up to the dream of the other. Yes, something like that. Something that cuts into us, remember when all of us had an into? and how rare they have become. When love wants to live up to the dream of the other.

It was a bridge burning not out of spite but out of preciousness, and she crossed it in a moment as brief as it took to form and if you map out her life, if you were to stretch and see the instant when north shifted its own compass, it would appear as nothing greater than an oasis, or a hidden grove. Yet beyond scrutiny there is a country and the sky is so tall here. There are places reserved for only those that reserve them. Do you see? Do you yet understand what they are trying to do with the other? When love wants to live up to its own dream.

Imagine a glistening that catches itself on morning. The doors are open, so you see; and if I can write you to me, let me beacon, and now imagine a silhouette beyond the glass and it knows more about you than anyone else ever will and the atmosphere is thick with it, and the chair is placed so perfect so that you can hear nothing being said but you know there are migrations of words that are meant, you close your eyes now and grip the thigh and somewhere there is a truth being lived and feel it now moistening your lips with the temptation to taste what they taste and the grain of their shapening is the taste you never taste and why stop so suddenly now, before you ask them, before you see them for what they have kept and you just stand up simply and let them know?

Song tied evenings canopy above them. The spring spent in Montana and she is a mountain. There were limbs crossing the aftertaste of my vision, and you are harbinger, and you are what you are welcoming. And their will be, after they be come what they have gathered this spunlight to form. It is impossible for them to describe unless it was a constellation they could have sculpted. Asking, what taste did you want this dream to become? Knowing there are forests in the heart you grow in me, and winter only arrives as a guest, with nervous feet, never knowing truly what to say, and what to see.

so sings my soul;

  the moon, the moon.

and I dream of dreaming of

  the chorus of your skin

  reflecting purples as a

gliding thing and to the

west   a footfall,

  and my beloved.

though time is stolen; a knife

  in the dark, small heart, time

is blessed be my love my Venus

  teaching; I let the rivers know

   you, blessed be, the Oak

and Eucalyptus sing in hollow

  browns and jade; she is

waiting, she is gold, blessed

  leaves.

though this concrete knows no

  echo, I will drum it; place

your ear elsewhere, where the

God of free things has kept

  them free; I will drum it,

and your heart is what this pulse

is for; here where the God of

caged things has kept them free,

I will dance, soundlessly, grateful,

in water and strong.

I negate this distance with

    what   it   would   be

    to be shining you.

there are grasps gathered in

    the corner of this thought.

    we have

            induced the splendor so

          rapid;   the tiny bird presented

          beneath my tongue   still

    panic and a heart for the weather.

still shuffling through the ghosts to

    ambush all joy and repeat.

the parking lot uses noise to become empty

    and I have these stories of coming home

    and so many homes that have came into stories

    yet the whisper still wets the morning

    shadow of what-will-my-skin-become today

  and with all these mysteries how does one create

    the swift of eye and soft of love?

I would lay you down between these captions of light.

and along the underwrist, you see where the

warmth is a visible knowing?   against that desert

of your body, my temple would press, and I would

begin to speak, simply, laying that way there beneath

your settling sounds.

when I see you

    there will be this moonline I

stand in.

a bedside lamp lit quickly out of sleep.

there are these places on your poem,

    where I want to write bodies.

    and learn the names of wind,

    (often asking the names of things.)

      by giving wind a name.

often replacing distant colors with the

    reflect of your allness and the chime

    of shapes.

And I wonder what you would find if you held your breath. I've wondered through the writing guessing at the height of your heart, at the still of your morning. I can shape these dreams through consistency into the pillars of the gentle place.

As though they forgot the other while on the path to each other. But her face once turned to his and these are important things and he says your face is perfect and it is impossible for him to describe his being without mentioning the lack of her. He measures himself by water; what was once full, now receding slowly into some fabled rumor of the what was that other way, that once, we, as in, we, found, stolen? It may have been. But you could have had the best of me.

What we surrounded. Sundrench, everything; secluded gestures they protect as their own eachothers. The things she desired to fly for him.

She wondered how to repair the break in her voice when she said his name, and how long it would take, for the guards of her border to notice.

She remembers her body. She remembers her body half submerged in the river. She stood, a single hand on the boat, he looked down at her, he looked off into the trees.

I can't understand what I understand, she built, But there is this mountain in me... And it's always been so quiet, but it doesn't want to be.

He seemed tired. Anger always made him seem so young.

She builds again, Why won't you just let there be light? She begins to cry.

She remembers. She tries to recall how many decisions in her life have been made while she stood halfway between two worlds.

There was once a writer, they loved each other without reason until they learned the reasons.

One morning they woke in Colorado and she stood in front of the window while the dawn watched. He looked: the pale curve of her lines, the hemisphere of what she changed.

I love the way you always let there be light. How it is before creation, your body is a genesis.

She wonders what becomes of people who say such things.

She misses all the things she used to let. Surrounded by those who sought beauty she would blush with the inner mine song that beauty was seeking her.

Maybe I've been in the city for too long, she thinks. A mountain living in the shadow of buildings.

The last time she made love to the writer was beneath the redwoods and free. She fell on him with tongue and faith, with a strength so strong that is chooses softness. She rose above him, half his, half theirs, and all her own. He was the water beneath her letting go. She stared off through the limbs and limbs and came as though in prayer.

And he let her.

We have walked this song before. I can taste myself on honeysuckle, sometimes in the air, or between the legs of gifts, as though, haven't we passed by this very same tree before? as though, are we not surely lost? as though, maybe we should just decide to create this place in the image of who we want to become and I will stare at you and you will stare at me and let us let it become important.

I want to strike the thing. I want a grip that is sure. I want more goodness to be required of me. See them, inner prostrate, daring the globe to test them, just to know, just to believe.

She tests the fullness of his mouth by trusting the words enough to swallow. They shape birds between their teeth; birds that sweat, birds that reach upward and feed off what they see. No one has been this way before, she says, watching him draw the equator of her breast with a purple pen. We have to be cautious in each other, I think we have entered some wild rib or marrow, something untamed and wary for survival. He nods, calculating the rivers of her throat with the coast of her lower back. He says he may have found a way, but it is hard to know, the stars are different when I am inside you. She nods. Maybe we should stop closing our eyes. They nod.

the arc of the letting go,   collecting

   glances between glass she loved and

   fabric faded in the light of their glow.

she can count on one hand,   where

   his hands have been.

there   is   this   burden they force

   to pearl between their tongues.

she orbits the room; cleansing

  constellations with the unseen line

 of his dream.   where are the shallows

   here?   where is this –safe place

step soft I've been near before, you

  can- what?-   trust, and tell me

  your name please   I want to say it right.

the space between   them was their own

   to feel.   somewhere near   there is a soul

at work;   scrying the hands with the wait

 of their hands.

and all of oneness gentle with the clocks

   they kiss goodnight.   he searches shadows

along the coast of her sonnet mouth.

they know the way.   the furniture is giving

 speeches.   the light is autumn bending to

retrieve a bookmark heavy.   this is the

   heart of it; her hand glides over his

shoulder as she leaves the room untended.

he knows the door is shut.   she is merely;

   refilling their drinks, changing her hair,

   everything, collecting empty pockets

   so they will always have enough.

he waits.   he hears the water running and

   cannot tell if her skins are being washed

or the rivers locked within her throat are

finally through with being denied.

the door opens, and the space between them

is their own to fill.

eye contact honey with all the harvest of

these lives they fit between the dawn

and moon. haunted by the moment passing,

such gifted context,   given,   with every

other   option   life   could   have   held.

do they count the weight between them

as all else that may have been? gratitude to

truly be   here   and   with.

he wonders where her love goes when it

wants to be alone.   asking seems sacrilege

with the color so close to flush.

mornings etch with the silence into

   the rib of this hand-like-drum-like tremendous

patience growing and restiform; circling my

   teeth with the tradition of moons.

the air seems calloused.   and while we stare,

  there is a throughness so present; while

you tongue the heart of me and cast these

   clouds so gentle.

who would I tell if not for you?

what shade of gift, does the lower lip,

  bring upward, everytime the doors

   close without you safe and secure?

I wanted to find it. I wanted the grasp to deserve what it held, you see, you weren't there, but we were the very hearts that redefined the thing.

Dear next thirteen miles, would you mind if I just continued to stare at how much life has already passed us by? And if you could ever begin to love my shape I would be honored if you would shape me, into something that finally will fit. Something that has earned its own name. I love when there is a celebration in me... I know these monuments that have built myownself and daily we find these tattered lights still touching the recluse reflection humming toward us and asking if we would like to return to some innocence that is gentle because it understands. Their love was gentle because it understands and lift your

Skies she says, are for us, and he has open hands, watch them, open, and she wonders what texture his thoughts would most closely resemble and she wants to add to love by knowing and she wants to see the world while knowing and what they are to the other changes the tastes of these breaths and here here have you seen this she says, have you seen how much more I love this knowing that it once loved you? This is important he says, life is for important things and they cover it with the other to protect it, and the other.

Other yards, a small fire stutters into the evening and he touches this place on her wrist and people are telling stories and they listen and he keeps touching this place on her wrist and the moon above them is true and the lust for these realities is dangerously true and she gives him that place and he touches it and all around them the night is being true and his hands, watch them open, close and everything is a promise forward, everything is something sown and they fucking notice that about being alive and they gift it to the other in a furry of thoughtfulness that is both jarring and perfect. Her mouth dawns the crest of an obscure sincerity and

Nowhere hidden has ever turned away a goodhearted guest. There are corners filled with chairs and the steam slow from the cup on the small lamp table and the sound of a distant city radiates and offers between the strokes of tiny bells. They long to become the hidden thing, to be found. The very gleam of the empty room seeks out a pulsing sun, the tone of dust and cobwebs await a letting go.

show them how you build.

    misdirected though you believe

    this wind may be.

and I've gathered hundreds.   I've

    grown a thousand more.

and this light to my mouth is spectacular.

heart quake still silhouetted for the

    best in us. the times told in cursive

      the script and heave of night.

promise to tell me of some small

    gentleness before I douse the light?

swear on this grip above that my

    shape is what you need.

if I could tend

    to the roots gentle in the

palm of your touch; gentle with the

  palm of my crest,   there would

    be quiets so loudly.

if these gathered sweats are allowed.

when you say,   those words

    that you say.

if light would direct nights without tremor

    or callous, we may find the valley

outside of this one or the other, that for

    such patience we have believed and

insisted that the echoes do indeed gather.

some mornings last the entire day,

    and in some existing vacancies the elsewhere

  sighs and rings its mighty knowing; love these

    questions, love the may have been.

if I held the sound of it

   for longer then you spent giving

than I'm sorry.

but   there are these

  learnings I love to trace

  again   while you

     held still to the

  main mast I swear it and

wave after wave isn't

  this what legs are for-

    for being

      held.   still

to the main mast I swear

  on wave after wave

 isn't this what heights

     are for?

I'll settle for histories.

  for that glass that you allowed

 to land so lightly.

  for that soft scent behind

your howl that weighs me.

Did she believe he had spent this whole time whispering just so she would be the one to define the thing? And after all that driving what did you want your heart to resemble after so many hours spent staring at mine? I can still wrap my hand around the hunger to love you. He finds it quickly, a distant pulse not so distant and behind his eyes he has storehouses of pollen and maybe you should churn here, patiently, awaiting, churn here, and let us swallow what our hands decided to desire to build by hand.

If these continents do drift at least we have direction. Watch as he creates gifts to give. Watch as she beckons his salvation with a mercy memory and now they gave these angels something to chase through the smoke filled windows of a city block they have learned to love.

There is another woman in their bed and they stare at her and with their sighs they ask each other, what is she when I am here, what am I when she is here, what are we when she is here, and they ricochet their light off her gathering weight and look at things again, practicing on the nearest star what someday may be required to believe, and when she stirs and sees them seeing and they ask her what are we to you when you are awake and she says you are a bridge, you are a sturdy phrase healing, you are the general surrendering because he is surrounded, but out of joy. They drawn her in, and forever there is this other place that is only for the crowded, and they bring what they have to share and they bring.

Sometimes he must negate this distance with what it would be to be shining you.

There was the legend of light and a perilous crossing. There had been a past tense that still gripped with an honor echoing beneath its surface story.

She walked beyond these arced borders and there were names carved in the flesh of trees from the time of Nomoon. No one mentioned these bridges we had abandoned for the dark swim, but there are kisses of salt that haunt the line of our neck. As hard as we try it's impossible to not forget.

The King had been ill since the first day. A sickness shaped in clock dreams still passed through him with copper hands; the blood was sad, the heart turned blue, the city filled with the music that broken stars play.

He has never satisfied the forest. There is a hallow above him that is holy. There are these spaces you may cleanse beside. The leaves on this path are bent, the winter laid down so suddenly. We have never been caught by surprise but it has been our benefactor at a distance.

Sometimes it would seem that even these very rocks are aching for something genius and brilliant to be. And the witness is holy.

But that last evening, the city square swelled with the populace, the burning buildings, the vehicles abandoned and turned on their sides; and the Wounded King; clad in the shadow dream that was paganism rides into the realm of our catastrophe. They watched a crippled veteran stand and clench his jaw with dignity, there were animals kneeling between alleyways and concrete. And there was this dream sobbing in the breast of her compass for the sake of magic. Oh for magics sake.

But in the gardens place, she glimpses against his tender showing and his thumb crosses her cheek and when they turn toward the other like this we all begin to love it and when the maps they have been feeding each other finally stain everything they touch they will touch and be stained and to want to accept everything, and to want to let it flood you, let it flood me, can we find any other form of being where we are entwined so tide shape and deepening? If we were to erase each other with one another and begin again, would the wind ever form more of a gratitude than the thanksgiving our come and intent celebrate? I have held these pages, the ones for you, and here we are, where they have us.

crest the thought of you and let it light:

the dream may have been stolen,

but you could love the best of me.

I've named you vibrant, and however

I basked in you once.

and I love what believes that love is believing.

if I hold your breath across the neverglance,

if you trust my eyes; this country

could resemble this.

can you   near me.   could we

hear   each other   strain to

brace   the   other:

along the milky night walk tender;

all touch a stowaway with wet eyes

and our humble hermit of inner splendor,

may sing toward you, may sing

toward me.

and I believe in your hands for what

    they could hold: moonbeam,

me steady, the dandelion of

   your voice.

something resounding open; somewhere

   distant, a kiss without hesitation,

a fragrance that reminds you that

  someone is awaiting your

     familiar joy.

as though you stared, into the sun, only

  for a moment, and forgot what you

  had woken here to say.

they never forced the city to unravel

  for them.   she holds her hand out

the open window;   one by land,

    two by sea.   and if some hollow

awaits their arrival, it has kept it

  very secret. if her fingers pause

at his mouth, she has kept it.

she must tell him before the next

   song ends. it ends. she forgets to

want. she tries to want. this is impossible.

   she, still worried, can he know

the bend of a neck under foreign breath?

   she almost asks, they are vibrant,

she does not ask.

the dashlights announce nothing; flush of

  skin -memory rising to the surface-

shift as you sense the lie, everpresent;

   you were never who they said you

   were. also, you were never who

   you said you were. but, you

   were someone, with so much to say.

and she touches him and it isn't a lie.

   he calls the static out of her

    and she heaves in a choir and it isn't a lie.

 but cast in smallest deaths, she

sighs and never speaks, and the moon is

     still to blame.

he spills the glass and he is sorry and

    she cannot hear him say he is sorry

and he begins to clean -but no oh no

   let me- and guilt is so difficult to

believe through.   and after all these

 glasses and she wonders if the city

will notice; if some allotted grace of

    arrival will be suspended in midyell,

midshine, and notice that the heart is

  not pure, though the love may be.

(hour: too dark, too dark. waking with static eyes,

    summer mouth.)

she: "I think it came from that way."

(earlier: nervous dinner, hurtful words. she went

    to bed before him.)

he: "Can you remember where we put the light?"

she: "I'm not sure. When was the last time we used it?"

(earlier: a new job, a new city. a choice is ripping

    through their story.)

he: "It is so hard to find things here. The moment you set

    something down it disappears."

    he finds the light: turns it on and off; a burst of seeing;

    blankets at low tide, she blinks in the shallows and it is

    dark again.

(suddenly: they remember.)

(hour: the front door opens and the world stretches

    beyond them like a sigh; thinning at every edge.)

(suddenly: he remembers other winters, breath just as

    grey, just as between them.)

she: "It must be near by, hidden in something close."

    he sweeps the light back and forth along the

    edge of the house. they search what they can

    see; their eyes, like moths that have grown tired

    of the chase.

she: "I could have sworn it was here."

he: "Nothing ever waits to be found."

she: "...I know for a fact that that isn't true."

(earlier: the year they first met, the way the windows would

    fog.)

(hour: she just put her arm through his.)

he: "Could it just vanish? That quickly?"

she: "It seems we would have at least noticed."

he: "How can you be sure? We didn't notice when it arrived?"

she pulls her arm out of his and turns away, a hand covers

her mouth; her hair is a mess, a mess he knows.

she: "But when something leaves...You should notice shouldn't

you? Something should be different."

he: "And what is that difference?"

there is a sound, he aims the beam,

focused, barely listening.

(hour: those moments that can change everything.)

she: "It depends...I guess, on how much space it took, or how

much space you gave.. That is the only time you find the total,

the sum is what is not there."

he: "I think we found it."

(earlier: he faced down cities for her; friends and family, miles and

debt. he pursued her beyond the limits of her own unbelief.)

(hour: she remembers the pursuit.)

she: "There is only so much you can truly love you know? The

weight of it, the hours it eclipses and never returns, you have to choose how to spend your heart so carefully."

he: "Wait...can you hear it?"

they both hear it.

he: "Its alot closer than we think."

she: "That's what I'm talking about."

he: "What?"

she: "Fullness."

they move toward the sound; quiet steps, light

off but ready.

(next door: he sees their flashing light, he wonders

what they are looking for, he wonders

how long they have searched for it.)

he: "We may have to surprise it."

she: "It may have to surprise us."

she is right, it was only the wind.

he: "It was only the wind."

she: "Are you sure?"

(suddenly: he realizes.)

he: "No..No it had to be more than just the wind."

(suddenly: her smile is such a grateful offering.)

she: "Are you sure?"

he: "Of course, after all this time, it is too real

      to be just the wind...I mean we are standing out

      here aren't we?"

she: "Yes, we would never be out here together if there

      were no reason."

he: "What is our reason?"

(slowly: against the side of the house. against the earth.

      over the handrail.)

(hour: back in bed, the blankets have risen and flooded over the

      way the night began.)

she: "We still have to choose you know."

      (slowly: he overwhelms her. a kiss of giving,

          a kiss of being offered. she moans and

          it is more than the wind. she takes his

hair in handfuls and it is for more than

direction.)

(hour: after.)

he: "We already have."

the room goes quiet. the body has released a

day of gathered sun.

she: "Earlier, where did you find it?"

he: "In the same place it always is."

(our view of the room is the single eye of the camera propped on the distant side of the table. the top of the table stretches long and finds her. the camera does not move. she sits at the end, we see from her neck down to the table. there is a glass almost empty and a cigarette case and a white lighter. there is light coming through the door, or window; the table is cut into slivers by the light.

it is quiet. no music. as little sound as possible. A weighted quiet, she is the only thing free of it.

her story should be as tired as the light is, and just as true. she needs to match the dusk with tone and knowing; she has to be aware that this story has been told before.

she has to have admitted that this is something she carries.

she takes a drink from the glass. sets it back down. her hand holds the glass. thumb rubbing something that isn't there, the glass should have been lifted from where it rested in shadow and be set down in the center of a splinter of the light. her hand strays to the cigarette case and the she opens it slowly, but closes it before removing one. she sets it back down.)

(a few moments pass. almost too many.)

"He told me....He told me that he found me because of my voice. But later, after that first rain and the laughter, he said that he felt that there was a book hidden between us. Some small thing lodged between a rib or a summer. And He wanted to find it."

(She picks up the lighter and absentmindedly rolls it in her hand before setting it back down.)

"It seemed that we met while gathering strength and momentum to finally surround and ambush the dream, (She sighs, tired.) We wanted to burn with something that was more than just a waiting."

(a door in the distance opens and shuts. A way into a room, not a way outside.)

"Living in Los Angeles was like entering a river willingly and then realizing it swallows you up forever. In the land of dreamers, it can be so difficult to dream. But I was getting better roles than I ever had, and his books were getting noticed by the right people, but not many. We were on that precipice of a life that requires you to leap or spend forever regretting..

I remember the first time he came to see me perform. I was in the dressing room; overfilled with flowers and cards. But when I picked up his gift; a small tin of breadcrumbs and a note that said "No one wants to find themselves at 60 wondering 'what if?'... When I read that, I knew we both had leapt without choosing to. That the heart read the Rorschach of a world and decided to cling to another throe of wonder."

(She picks up the lighter again and sets it down fast. Almost angry, but never loud.)

"One night, we found ourselves heart deep in a fever. I had received my worst review yet from a critic who seemed focused on destroying everything, and he was three weeks gone from writers block...We both understood that sometimes life slows, and sometimes it stops, and everytime it would, hand in hand, we would leap into or toward some new tributary. Forcing the circle eight to snap by hunger alone. We got into the car and drove east.

We always ran away to find each other..."

(she pauses. Hands are still. Suddenly she leans over and picks up some scrap on the floor. Her face passes through the camera view but just for a moment, it is the only time we see her face. She is close to tears. Her voice and speech pick up an almost frantic momentum.)

"There are things I miss and things I never want again, but what I loved about him... love about him, was that everytime the dream would suffer he would try his hardest to overwhelm it, to make it fucking beat again. He told me he wanted to see how I sounded in the desert, we stopped at dusk and shoved our hands into the still warm sand and he kept saying 'this is what it's like, this is what it's like' and I could feel it beat, I could feel its surprise at its own depth... (she calms down, breaths, hands go still again.) I fell asleep while he drove without a destination and a trusted him."

(another, or the same door opens in the house, we hear footsteps, we maybe see someone pass by, a pant leg or a sleeve. Or even just the light and sound from a door opening and leading outside, and shutting. She is quiet, calmed. The air is nervous.)

"We got to Paducah Kentucky, my family has a house there. We stretched and breathed the new air of a new day. There was a light fog still keeping things secret, yet slowly revealing all. He walked between the tombstones that tell my story and he read each one out loud. We slept all day, he said the southern air made my skin taste like persimmons."

(Quiet again. She can tell the that the story is almost done. Her voice tilts and weaves.)

"That night we drank too much. We talked about heaven, and he talked about voices and there was something about this place that broke my heart. My blood is filled with constant yearning and a lifetimes worth of nights filled with fireflies that I've never had and maybe it all began as something stolen but I told him that my story led to here and I've never played this part, I haven't even read the lines. But when I stepped out of that car and the wind was curious around me and I looked at him and said 'this is what it's like, this is what it's like.' "

(She is quiet. Maybe crying. It may be hard to tell.)

"I told him I had to stay. I told him he wasn't allowed to stay. That love was not ending, but that I needed this, and trusted him to not withhold it...he understood. He wasn't going to go home. LA would destroy him alone, I understood. He left the next morning, searching for a city with light that reminded him of me. He would mail me empty envelopes and boxes, I would take them into my closet, shut the door, and quickly open them. A flash of foreign light would fill the room, but only for a moment. I would whisper 'this is what we're like, this is what we're like.'...

It may have begun as something stolen; my life is a testament of how brightly life can overtake you; in a closet, or a desert, or in the fragrance of persimmons without a source. I haven't seen him in three years, but I've come close. I read his books, I know when he writes only for me. From time to time I can still find breadcrumbs in the crack of my voice, or in the warm air long after the sun has set...He was right. The wondering 'what if'....it's like this."

It may not necessarily have a thing to do with freedom but there are moments in my life where I believed I truly heard something. Once, around a crowded table of strange women, my friend and I witnessed a single voice rise above the din by declaring that 'The thing with iguanas is, that iguanas are free.'

And I'm not saying we haven't been hurt. I don't mean that at all. But in the midst of blue eyed instants and liberated iguanas it appears that a life has begun to form. I cannot point you to the genesis, but I believe the trail head rests soon after the dawn when they first realized they were wearing no clothes.

When your hand moved from my hand to my elbow, I finally understood wind. The trace you leave behind resembles the parable but releases all marrow slowly, the light falling together like tumblers in a lock and the door opens on its own accord and everyone sets down their glass and wonders how long that has been there.

She told me there was a place on my face she wanted to inhale. When the sun broke through today for just a moment I held my breath; marinating in a souvenir of spring, trying to retain the burst of summer so that if winter takes its time, I will have something to give, when she begins to lean into me and give.

When the air is sharp and the moon is your middleman and if you decide to run in a field naked, you should be careful of headlights. You should be careful to only howl when it fills you, or else you will know it was a fake, you really will, I assure you.

If there is a creek, or a fallen log, I would recommend a leap, a pounce. Landing crouched low with your fingers in the earth. There is something hidden, in the earth, in the pounce, that maintains a dignity beyond social history. When you land, everything seems so wild, and you welcome it.

Somehow the two are connected. Her kindness, her night, and the running. I haven't pinpointed the limb that ties the root of this to the fruit of her, but maybe one day, if the reptiles defend their kingdom, we will set down a single glass and look at the years between now and then, and wonder how long that has been here.

If you run naked through a storm it is much different from running through a light rain. One adds a calm violence, you allow your feet to grip and push. The other resembles a playful waiting, a hushed impatience. I'm not sure which is which, but these seem to be the options.

If you have to wear shoes you can. But is isn't the same.

I hold my breath and somewhere the mud is the

    softest and my hands search for the things that

strangers lose. I try and define that distance,

the horizon and a neglected keepsake: I attempt

    to hold that in and taste how full the thought

      is, I will try to love   these small mouthfuls

    when everything is a sea.

the dusk is a child that interrupts out of wonder.

    I'm laying hold of the part of their story

  where he must be believed in, to ever

believe again. I'm surrounding that insistence

  and calming the tattered edge; the fray of

    what you thought your time would be.

what you had hoped your heart would resemble,

    floating here, as lovely as it is naive, still

    waiting for the echo of one hand clapping

 across the shadow your daydreams cast

    over your success,

and you know she is out there being someone

    beautiful and you know there is always a sky

    and some of these souvenirs are too real

  to be memories and I imagine what you would

find if you held your breath.

windows fill with light

    and crouching beneath the

lower corners we drink

    the excess spilling over.

you hold the spines of leaves

    in the air and of

    all the ways I admire

you, I prefer on my

    knees   and

someday your stomach will

   swell as we design

echoes   and when

   we hold our ears to

the night and ask

   who,   who?

it will be you

   who has this magnificent

reach.

mikl paul is 29 and lives on the central coast of California with

his wife BreEle and their overweight cat. This is his first book

published. He spends his time watching.

This is the first book published by Olivia Eden Publishing. They are
located out of California and are currently in the process of releasing a
collection of short stories by various writers and also an anthology of
fairy tales by talented friends and strangers from all around the globe.
Thank you for helping us attempt to keep books brave.

oliviaedenpublishing@gmail.com
www.oliviaedenpublishing.com

www.ingramcontent.com/pod-product-compliance
Lightning Source LLC
Chambersburg PA
CBHW081523040426

42447CB00013B/3316